LETTER FROM THE EDITORS

HOME is a very difficult thing to build. You might be surrounded by an environment that is not allowing your voice and opinions to be heard. When this happens, you run to create a HOME that will not only value what you have to say, but you extend that acceptance and safe space to others. But then, just when you think you've finally created a HOME where you have worked many hours, days, months, and maybe years to create this strong foundation, you might encounter yourself with a wall that not only stops you from feeling you're valued and heard, but you end up tired, drained, and questioning your reasons of creating your HOME in the first place.

Dear readers, if you find yourself in this same situation, please run. Get out. It's no use wasting your energy on a HOME that doesn't value you as a person. Which is why for this issue, we focused on this very theme and invited collaborators to share their own experience with HOME. It might not even be a physical HOME. That's the beauty and ugly side of HOME. It can be anyone, anything, and any place. The advice I can give you, as someone who is also realizing that the HOME they built isn't what it's supposed to be and feels their own voice is being drowned by another, is that it's okay to leave and start over. It's okay to push aside destructive homes that make you feel empty at the end of the day - no matter the positive result or gratifying exhilaration it might give you.

I hope you find the strength to take that decision. Trust me, it's hard and it might take many months or years for you to make it. But once you take action, you won't stop smiling by having that heavy weight lift from your shoulders. So, please find solace in the creative work featured in this issue and once you find the light to pull you out of that awful tunnel, I hope you find the drive to build a new HOME where you feel safe, loved, valued and your voice rings loud and clear!

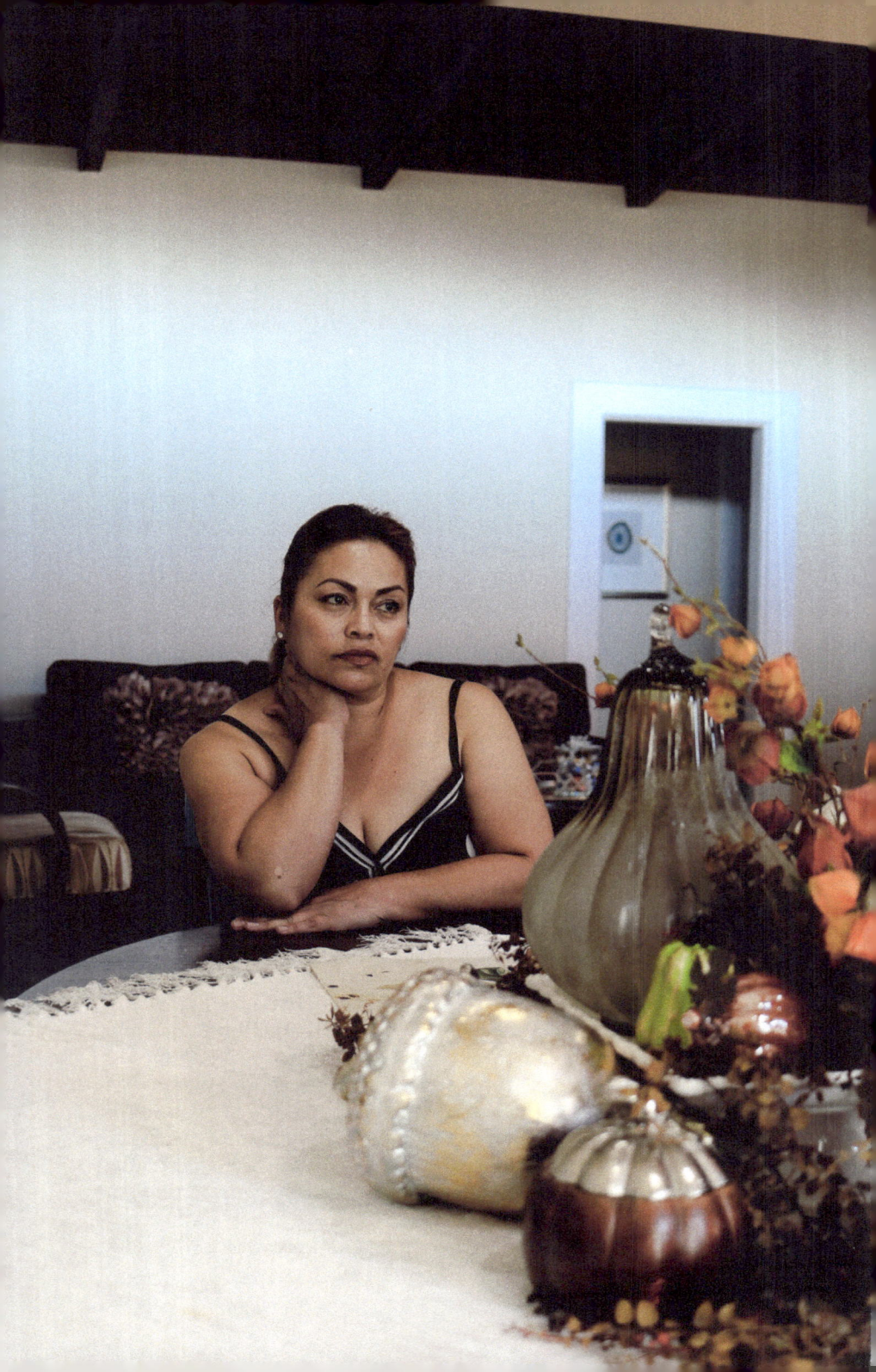

4	RUNNING HOME
11	DANCING WITH DEATH
15	COMO LA MONARCA
17	FLOAT WITH PIERRE VAN VUUREN'S STUNNING PORTRAITS
24	I WANT YOU NOW
27	THE VICE COLUMN

EDITORIAL SHOOT
Photographer: Josephine Jael Jimenez
Model: Susana Jimenez

RUNNING HOME

Josephine Jael Jimenez

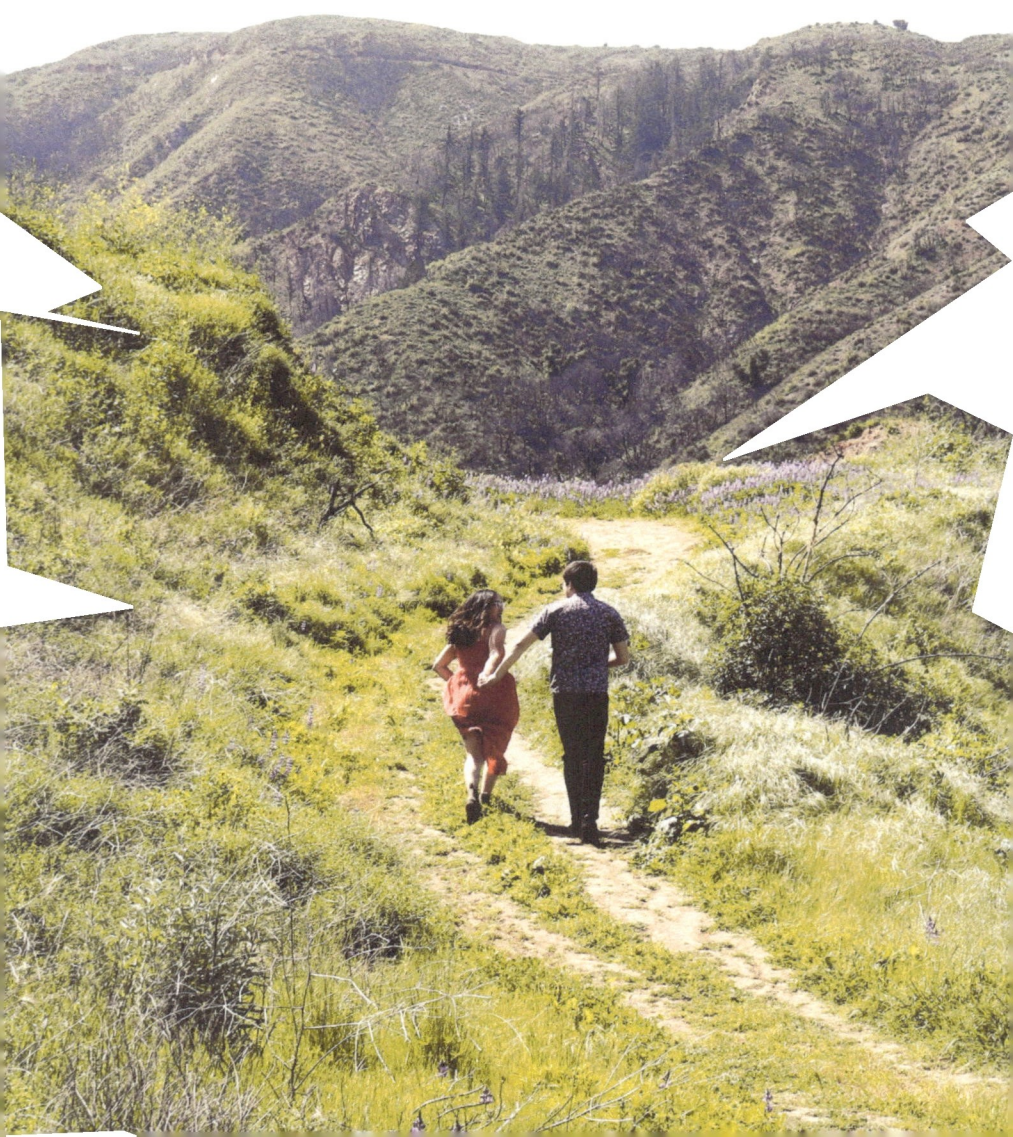

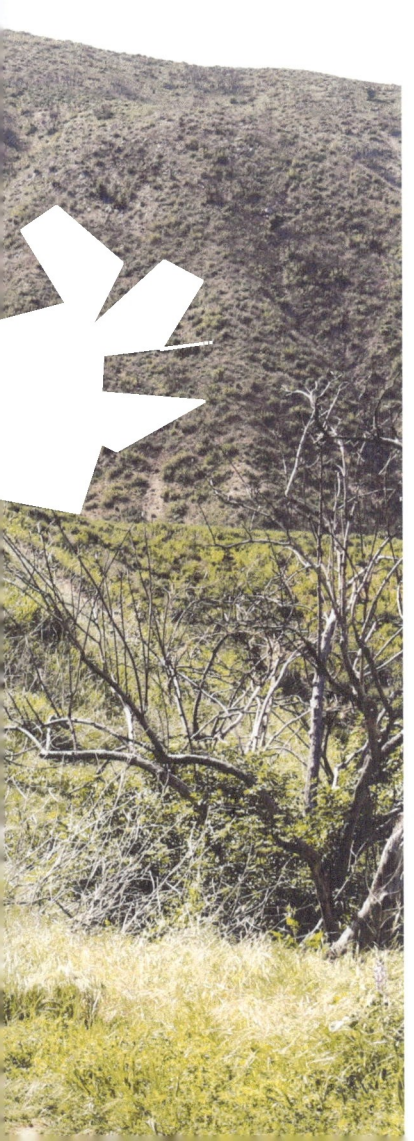

Traveling was the only running I've ever been able to do because in high school, I was hit by a car the first day I rode my new bike to school. I was mostly fine except for some pretty serious knee damage and a severely bruised ego. My doctor said my knee would get better over the years and would be greatly helped through low impact exercise like riding a bike or swimming a few laps in the pool. Well the universe doesn't want me riding bikes, obviously, and I'm scared of water, so naturally I did what any other injured and lazy person would do: nothing. Needless to say, I was never a runner, before or after the accident. Ironically, running was my biggest dream and my most seemingly unachievable goal way back in my childhood. Running in the metaphorical sense, of course. Hence the traveling. Sloppy solutions deserve sloppy introductions.

Over my "adult" years, I've traveled as much as I could in any capacity that was available to me and I fell in love with getting on a plane or hopping in a car and going somewhere new where life felt different and I felt the same. I wasn't running from myself, just the surroundings that tried to dictate who I would become.

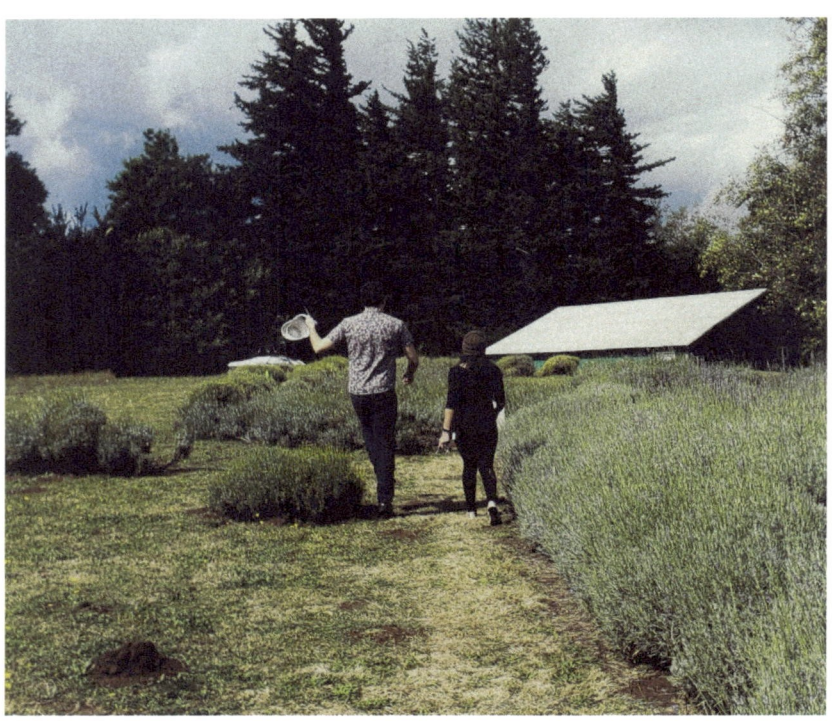

When I went somewhere new, there wasn't time for people or places or systems to tell me who to be or what to do, etc etc. Feeling like an outsider became comfortable. Making a home wherever I landed was easy and safe. Over and over again, I ran towards a feeling of home and belonging I couldn't cultivate in my every day. At least not without an immense amount of work.

That's what life felt like. Work. When I was in school, I had to work at that. Then I moved on to having jobs where you work all day for a few hours of respite at night and a couple of days off at the end of the week. There wasn't much room to make my life exciting in the work week, but when I was far away from the troubles of all that, I found rest. Even in the tourism and the meeting people and the general restlessness that is normal to travel, I found rest. My soul was rested and found its home in a peace I couldn't replicate outside of not being where I was always supposed to be.

And then I fell in love and all that changed.

Now I'm accountable to another human in a way I wasn't before. My everyday is shaped around another person and over the course of each of those days, I become more and more aware of how different it all is. My work week and my days off don't feel like they used to. I don't ache for home the way I used to when I was running towards finding it anywhere I could. I have a home that I love and that I cherish, but sometimes I still ache for the exact feeling I used to get when running was all I wanted to do.

· · · · · ·

There was a recent period of time where I couldn't travel. The time just wasn't there even though the desire always nagged at me. My soul ached for the rush of going somewhere new. But after that season was over came a season where my partner and I prioritized my desire to see the world, all thanks to a few airline sales and companion passes. But each trip left me even more tired than the last

"I don't ache for home the way I used to when I was running towards finding it anywhere I could."

and I thought my spark of home had finally left me. I couldn't regain the feeling I once had on these journeys through places I didn't know and I felt hollow.

It felt like I had traded one feeling of home for another when really I wanted to keep both. Maybe it's selfish to have a home but still want to crave the feeling of home, but I couldn't help it. That feeling felt like it was mine and it felt like something that kept my individual sense of purpose alive. What my partner and I have built is beautiful and filling, but it's ours. I wanted what used to be mine.

After the second to last trip, I felt like calling the last one off. Who needs to deal with airports and airplanes when the feeling you're looking for was nowhere to be found, but obviously I went anyway. The money was already spent and someone was waiting for us on the other side of that terminal.

The trip started off the same. We went through the same security line at LAX and got on a plane that was exactly like the others and flew through a sky that I didn't even bother to look at because it was going to look the same. The lights beneath us weren't so bright anymore, they just were. I didn't care about the cities beneath us and how small they looked and I didn't think about the atom sized people down there or wondered what they dreamt about while we were way above their heads, sailing through the clouds. I finished the sudoku puzzles in the flight magazine instead, while sitting in that seat with my back aching like it usually does and it all made me instantly exhausted. A whole weekend seemed impossible to get through, but I was already in the air with a ride waiting to come get me when the time came.

As soon as I stepped out into the fresh Portland air and the reality of seeing one of my oldest friends for a whole weekend hit me, I felt that twinge of home again. Nothing prompted the feeling, we were just standing there waiting for her to drive up in a car that was just like mine, but there it was. Home. Home. Home.

• • • • •

Over the weekend and the few days that I've been back from that whirlwind trip I've been trying to figure out why it felt so different. Why did that spark come back during that last trip? Where was it during all the others? What did I do right and what had I done wrong?

I realized my mistake had been comparing it to the trips I had taken this year and not the ones I had taken alone in years past, before

I was in love and before I started blending finances with someone else.

Back then I was BROKE. Much more than I am now. I traveled to places with very little money in my pocket and even less plans in my head as a result. Those trips were put together with rubber bands and bubble gum and there were plenty of people who thought I was crazy just for traveling as much as I did on my own, as a young fragile female. When they asked how much money I had in the bank, some people begged me not to go. But that feeling always called me back to risk it all.

Portland wasn't like that, though. We had money. I didn't really have to think about paying for food or souvenirs or the destination themed t-shirt I buy my dad no matter how little money I have wherever I go. We may not be rich, but my partner isn't as crazy as I tend to be. He plans his finances according to his plans, bless his soul. Home was never about how much money I did or didn't have, it was more abstract than that.

While visiting my friend — the one who had lived one street over from me for most of my life, the one who I spent multiple summers with hanging out at her family's home and the one who I had gone through those awkward middle school and high school years with — we had decided to take her and her boyfriend up on their offer of staying with them at their apartment with their amazingly cute pup. That was the difference. The difference that made home for me the way I had always worked towards was that simple. I had stayed at my friends' apartment.

On the other trips I had gone to this year, we had stayed in hotels, Airbnbs, or with people I didn't know all that well. On all the past trips I idolize in my head, I had stayed with people that I loved. To take it a step further, I had stepped into their lives for a while.

Because I was broke, most of my trips were to visit people I loved. Alabama, New York, Ireland, Maryland, Texas, blah blah blah. All this time I didn't realize that it wasn't really the travelling that my soul craved, it was the people and I feel stupid for not realizing that because my whole life, I had always felt at home with people.

My friend, the one I plan on keeping for the rest of my life, had invited me to her home. That trip wasn't about seeing Portland, it was about spending time with people who I loved and who loved me and seeing the life they had built and loving them in that world as much as I loved them in mine. This whole time I should have realized that it wasn't the newness that I craved (even though I still love it for what it is and plan on chasing that, too), it was the familiarity mixed with the expanding. It was loving the people I love even more.

It helps that I found home—a home I can hold on to forever—and a partner who will hold my hand during the scary in flight turbulence, but it's also sweet to know that I have so many other homes in the world. Maybe I've always known that, but now I know for sure and now I know where to point my feet.

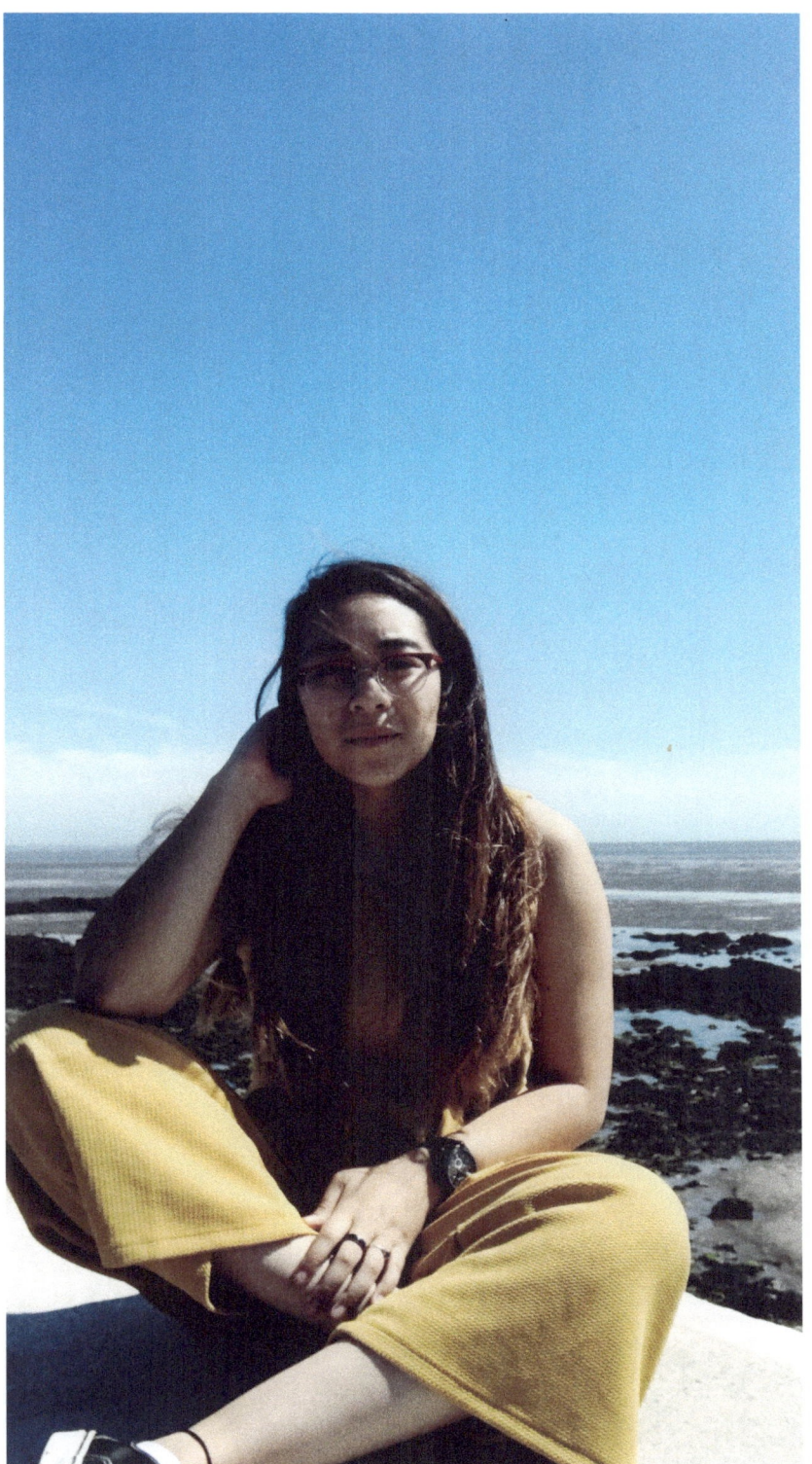

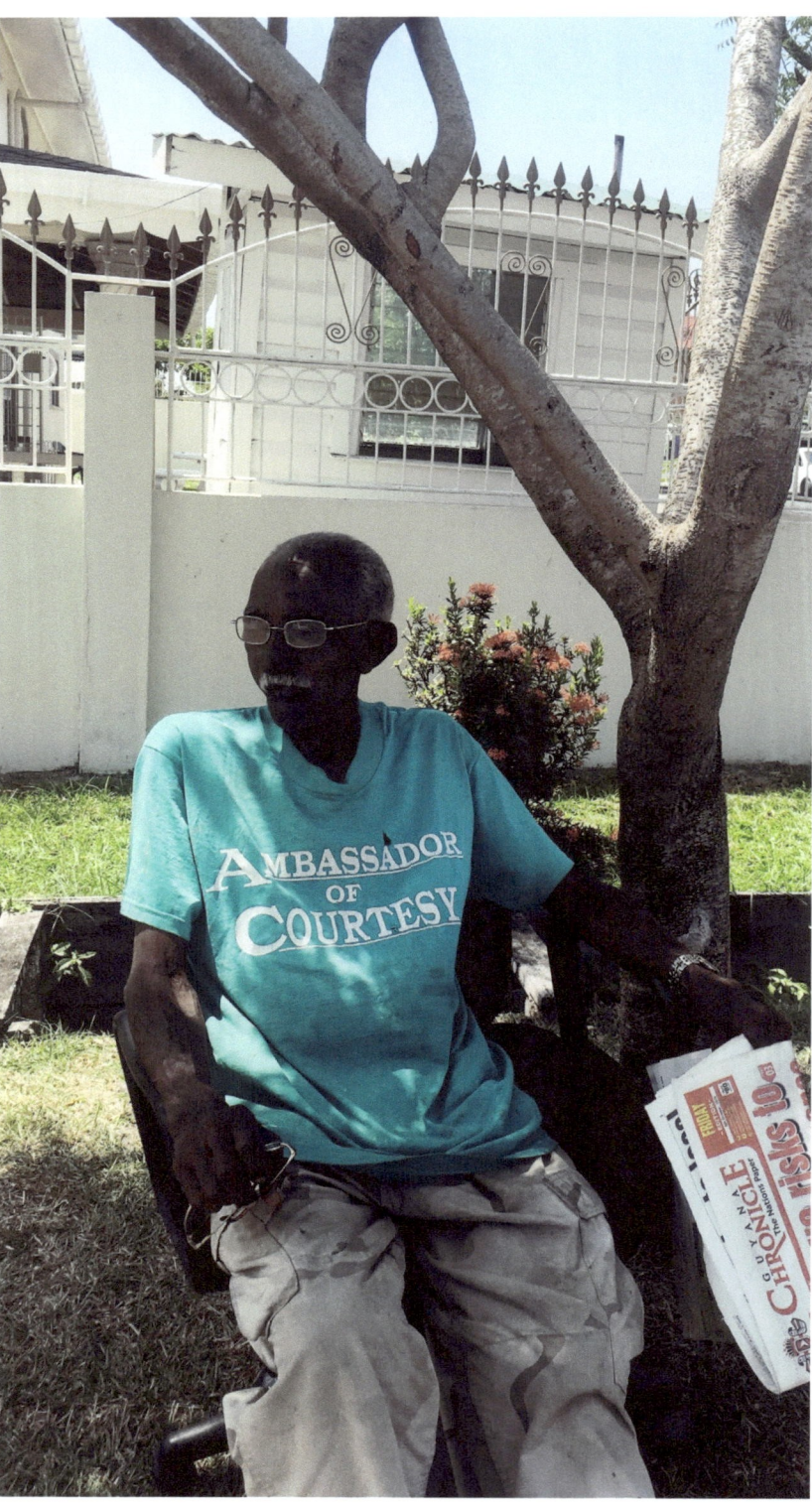

Dancing with Death

MARISSA BLACK

It was a few nights into the New Year when I passed along the box packed with rice, chow mein, and macaroni to a man nearby. These plastic to-go boxes were essentials at wakes in my new home of Guyana, and I scanned the yard to see that the friends and neighbors of the deceased had been served and were comfortable. Guests slammed down dominoes on little white tables and conversed with one another from plastic lawn chairs. The whole neighborhood crammed into the yard of this house on the corner. Gospel tracks and Caribbean Oldies crooned from the speaker boxes, a soundtrack for nostalgic conversations. This was my neighborhood.

Our elderly neighbor, Frenchie, had died in his sleep a few days before. A staple in the community, I could always count on him being settled in his folding chair on the corner, the daily paper and his dog, Guava, his faithful companions. He would stop every neighbor who passed by just to chat, taxi drivers honked their hellos to him, and old friends dropped off groceries for him and food scraps for Guava. So it seemed the whole city knew when he died. Bus drivers asked me where the uncle on the corner was. School children wondered about his absence. Every time I left my house, my eyes would flick over to his corner, expecting to see the sentinel posted in his chair. But now only Guava was there.

Frenchie was one of my first friends when I moved to the vibrant Caribbean country 16 months earlier. He was a constant in my morning commute. Many stifling, humid mornings I would sit next to him on his stoop, rest my bag on an old cable spool he'd turned into a table, and chat as I waited for my ride to work. And several hours later, on my way home, I would see him on his corner again, sitting, one knee crossed on top of the other, observing the road, waiting for someone to talk with. Maybe he would quote Macbeth verbatim, recount his drug-fueled twenties traveling abroad, or ask me to walk him to the shop for a lotto ticket or haircut. And every evening, in the Caribbean dusk, he waited up until he saw the first star come out so he could say a prayer when he saw it. Frenchie would tell me which of my roommates had already come home before me, who was still out, where they had gone, and whether they'd be back by sundown. He was the neighborhood watchdog and gossip. And he was the one who made this unfamiliar culture and new lifestyle feel like home.

And now, sharing out packages of food at his wake, I saw the entire neighborhood gathered in his honor. The men who played cards every night outside the tire shop, his landlady and house-mates, the man who weed-whacked the trench out front, the quirky locals who had known him for decades—these old friends, a few estranged family members, and neighbors gathered at the house on the corner to swap stories about the legend. I was fascinated by his friends' stories of Frenchie as a young man, but I could feel the weight of it all beginning to build up. Guyanese wakes can last for several nights, and I could sense my social energy draining on this, the third or fourth night.

Another Christmas away from my family had just passed, and adding the death of a friend to the already somber tone of the holidays was making the humid nighttime air feel even heavier. It was comforting to witness the gathering of neighbors in celebration of Frenchie's life, but I was physically and emotionally exhausted, letting myself indulge in some level of self-pity. I knew Guyana could never fully be my home, that I could never completely integrate into a culture that was not my own. However, I knew with equal certainty that the cities where my friends and family lived State-side could never fully be home again either. Building a cross-cultural home brings its share of excitement and joy, but it also carries stretches of loneliness and isolation. I don't really get homesick, but building a new community for myself every year or two can take its toll on your spirit. And now I had lost part of my home, my new community— someone who held his own community together.

And, standing in the yard of so many past conversations, seeing the room where they had found him, the stoop where we had waited for the stars, and flicking my eyes to his corner, I knew I needed to leave the death behind. My roommate always swore that after you leave a funeral or a wake,

"And he was the one who made this unfamiliar culture and new lifestyle feel like home."

you can't go straight home. You can't let the death follow you back. You must leave it somewhere else. There were plenty of things I needed to leave behind, and I knew just the place to go.

Thirty minutes later, I could hear the muted booming of the salsa and reggaeton tracks as I climbed the steep stairs into the Latin club. A haven. People of all skin colors and nationalities twirled and swirled and salsa-ed around the floor to Marc Anthony and Shakira. Cubans, Guyanese, and Trinidadians blended and jived together with North Americans sprinkled in. I generally balked at places that drew ex-pats and Westerners, but I knew that tonight this was where I needed to be.

In this new home, dance had become a tool for me—an invaluable instrument of expression and self-care. It became a way to deal with the stress of a new season of life, a new job, and new expectations. And tonight I knew I wasn't just there to leave behind the death; I was going to need to dance with it. I needed to face this loss, hold it close to me, and understand how it moved. So under twinkling Christmas lights strung up around this bar in the Caribbean, this place I had made a home, I danced with the death-scent. I stomped and spun and salsa-stepped. Ice cubes in nearby drinks vibrated to the rhythms of song and dance. I was dancing to understand—to know I lost a part of my home but not all. That night I wasn't dancing to push away Frenchie's death or to pretend it hadn't happened. I danced to grieve the loss of him. The loss of all the many homes and communities I had known before. And I danced to celebrate. To celebrate him, the home I had found, and the homes that are to come. I swung my hips in gratitude, rocked back and forth with loss, and flicked my eyes to the corner.

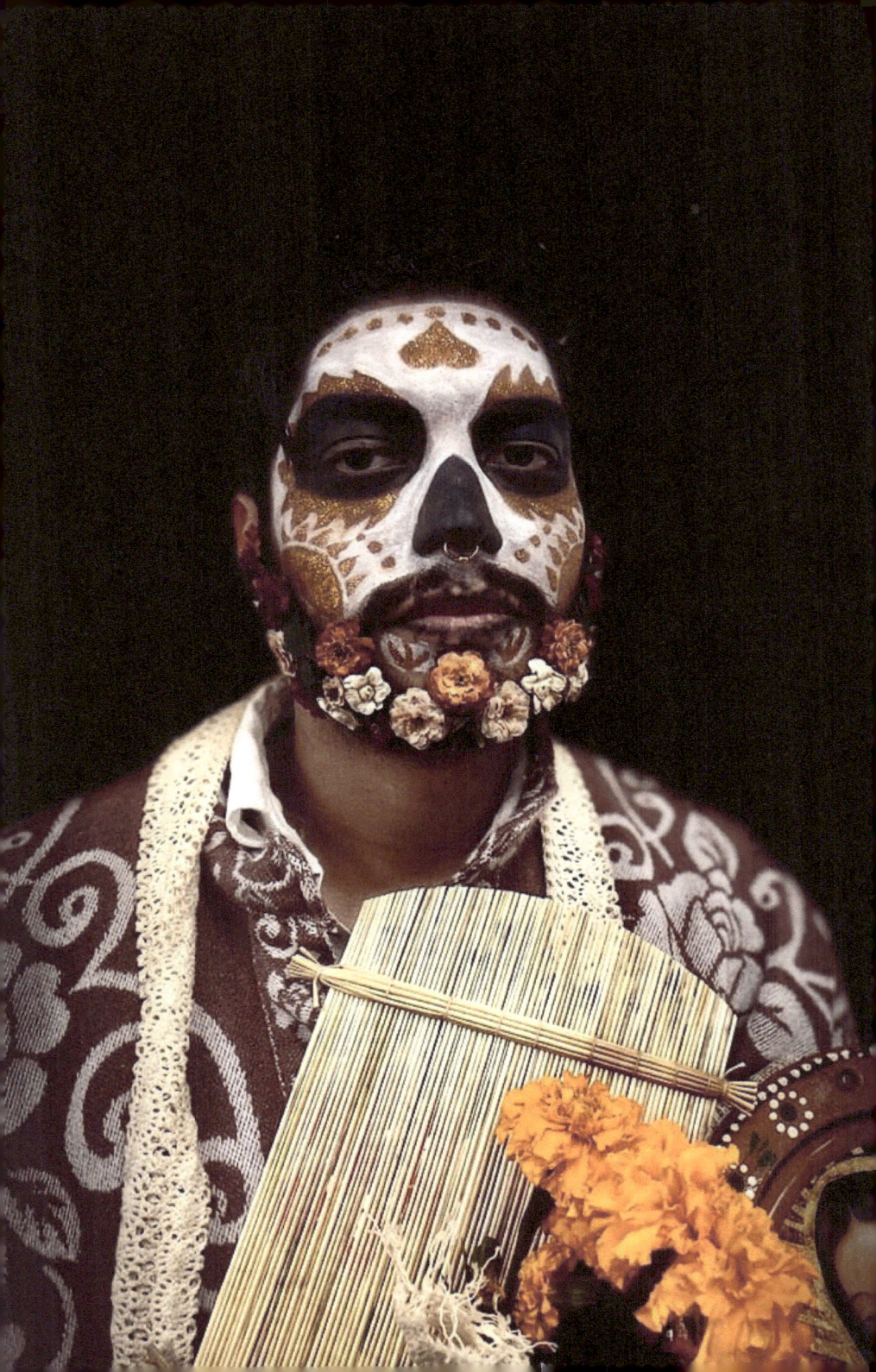

COMO LA MONARCA
JAVIER COVARRUBIAS

"Migration.
A journey in uncertainty.
A return to roots.

Like the monarchs carrying the spirits of the dearly departed back to our ancestors' native land of Michoacán, I too have found my soul restored to a familiar sense of self following a season of healing and delicate transformation.

Javier - castle; a new house
Covarrubias - red cave

From broken, bloodied wounds—
Rebirth.
Foundations fortified in stone—
Reconstruction.
Fundamental monarchy of self, sustained—
Reclaimed.
Freedom fulfilled in forgiveness—
Reconciliation.
Fearless reflection of my journey gives guidance towards my final destination—
Home."

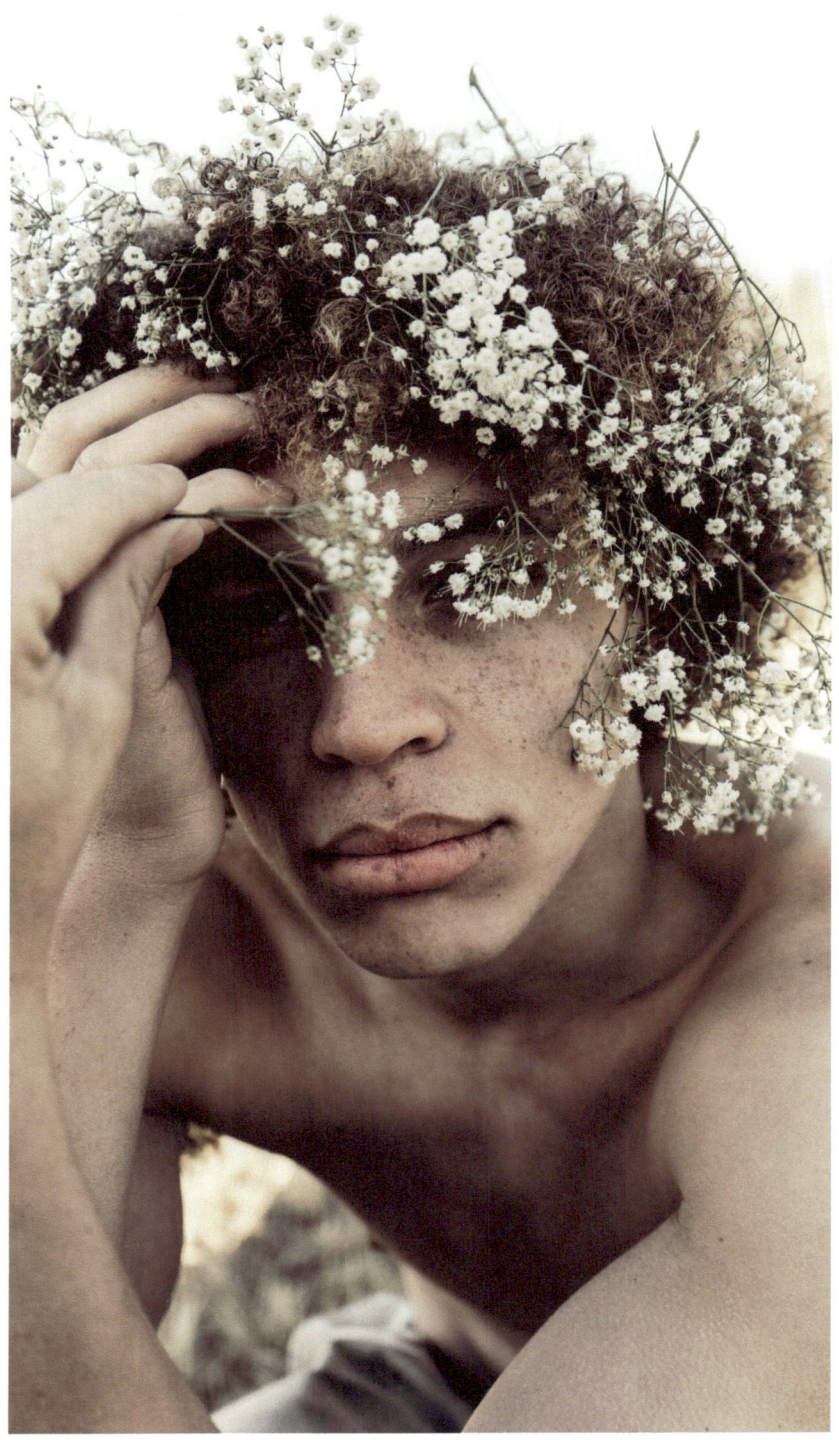

Float with Pierre Van Vuuren's Stunning Portraits

BRENDA HERNÁNDEZ JAIMES

If there's one thing I love, it's being bewitched by enchanting photography that overflows with endless enigmatic beauty. Pierre Van Vuuren's photos invite you to dive in and float in the stunning portraits he shoots. The visual expression that Pierre can communicate is a jewel box that holds love, joy, and a thrilling rush of emotions. As a young photographer from Pretoria, South Africa, Pierre has evolved both as a person and artist. He continuously pursues his path to refine his artistic eye and skills to provide valuable images that are filled with intention and a clear message to the viewer.

"My work has started having more of a story to tell and being way more intentional than it was before. Before I liked taking beautiful photos and still making art, but now it's way more intentional and it has a purpose," Pierre shares.

The series 'Flower Man' is Pierre's latest iconic work that rings true to his recent vision of creating artistic, beautiful, and intentional imagery filled with purpose. This change in his work is a result of his time in Canada where he was able to visit many art galleries and behold artistic photography that told a story. His creative mind was immediately captured and once he returned to South Africa, it inspired him to fine-tune his photography.

"The biggest thing about Flower Man is the story of how history has done a lot of cultural appropriation. The reason why I put the flowers in Jean Claude's hair is that some people see, especially in the past in South

Africa they decide what they like about the culture and race and then they appropriate it, but they don't take it in as a whole. So it was leaving a comment about that," Pierre states. "Because Apartheid was a thing, racism was a thing and it's still a thing. When I was speaking to Jean Claude about it and he's mixed race and in South Africa, it's called coloured and there's a culture around staying coloured. That was one of the first things where I had an idea and it came to life in the way I thought it would."

The message that 'Flower Man' communicates is clear and Jean Claude Myburgh's face being warmed by the sunlight and having his hair filled with baby's breath that symbolizes everlasting love, pureness and innocence speak loud and clear of the race, ethnicity, culture, and history in South Africa. As a young gay man, Pierre is also envisioning and preparing to create a photography series that revolves around the experience of gay men in the different cultures of South Africa. The conception of this project also comes from Pierre having his close family members knowing about his sexuality and being supportive.

"Hopefully it'll make waves in the country and it will speak about not being scared as a gay man to be feminine or act the way you are because of critique. Because that's the hardest part, there's so much controversy if you're a gay man and if you're feminine. It can be the truth, but it's not always the truth. It's not set in stone that if you're gay, you're feminine," he says. "Even now when I act in a

"Hopefully it will make waves in the country and it will speak about not being scared as a gay man to be feminine or act the way you are because of critique."

certain way, I'm like, 'Oh, Pierre, you're being too feminine.' It's always difficult."

"It's hard...and high school in that sense was very hard. In Canada, it was having a safe space in the choir and I felt so accepted there, so that has changed how I feel. When you realize you hate yourself for it, but now I'm not afraid to tell anyone and I'm open about it," Pierre shares. "When it comes to being gay and being bullied and I have a lot to share about growing up in a very conservative African culture. It's only recently when the younger generations have started to be more liberal about it. Going to Canada kind of made me see it how it should be in a country when

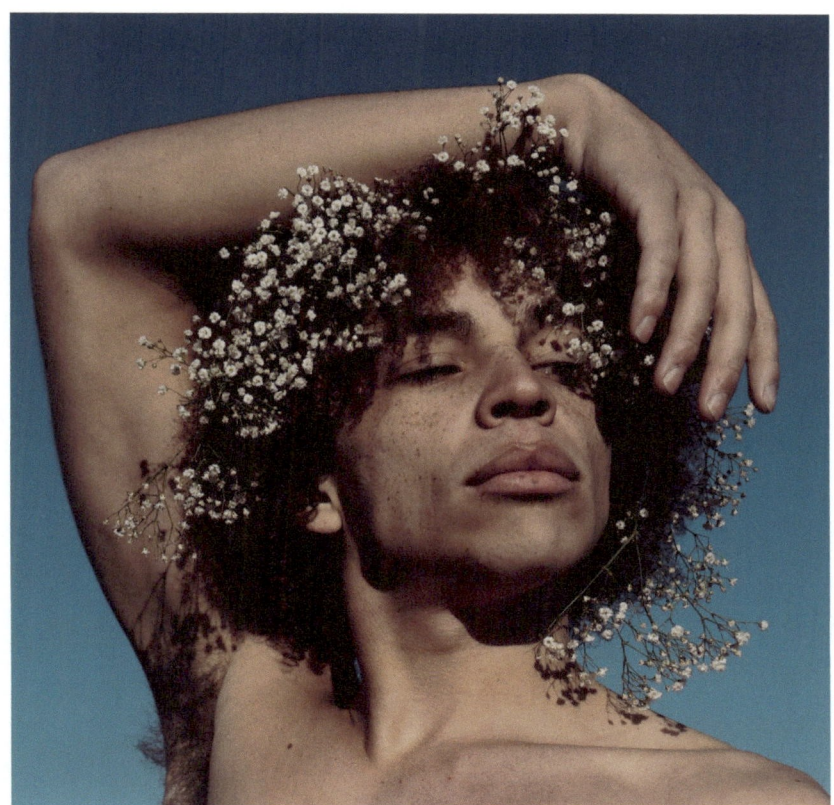

you're part of the LGBTQIA+ society and family. Because there it wasn't like a thing and in South Africa, it's such a big thing when someone comes out as gay. People still get bullied," he continues.

"I'm a Christian, but I'm gay, so it's very controversial for me growing up. When I was a teenager and made the decision, they tell you it's a decision, but it's more like a decision of trying to accept it. I had to be like, 'how am I going to feel about being gay and being a Christian? Do I let go of my faith?' And it's only later when I realized that I don't have to do it. It's part of me and people just don't understand it. My friends have been accepting, but I've been in situations where people haven't been very accepting and I want to tell a story about that. Especially being a South African, how I've experienced it" Pierre says.

The change if his photographic vision truly began to grow once he traveled to Canada to be part of the University of Pretoria Youth Choir back in 2016 and most recently in the beginning of this year. Pierre was chosen to be part of an exchange program with a choir in Edmonton, Alberta, for six months he sang in three different choirs, taught African music, and frequently traveled with the conductor. During his time in Canada, his photography went further to street photos, creating a clear message of his work, and perfecting his skills. Choir and

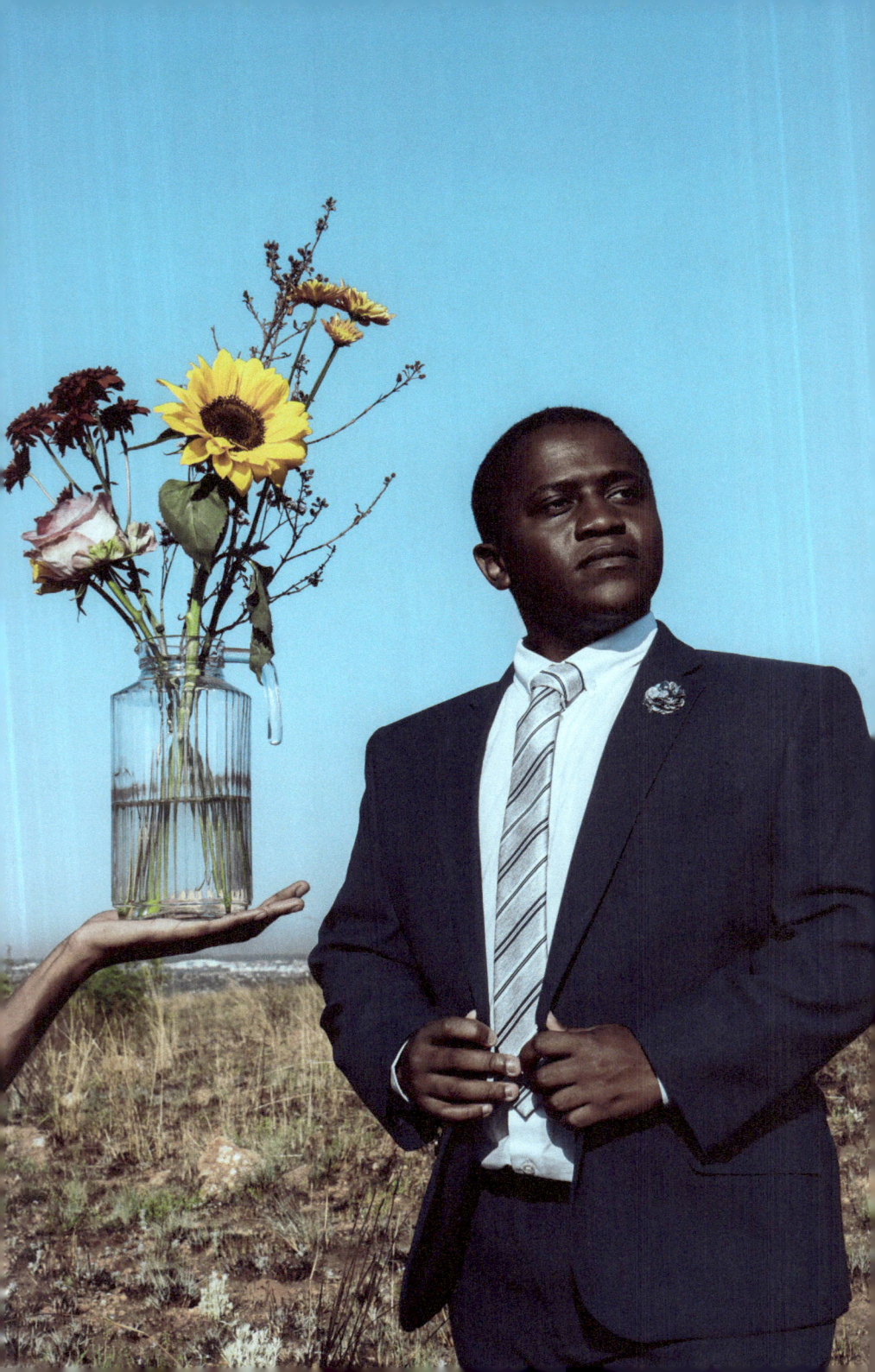

"I have to tell stories."

photography are two important factors that are part of Pierre's life that also provide him a safe space. Yet life is full of setbacks and finding your passion is sometimes discovered in these moments. After high school, Pierre took a gap year and had a job that had a draining environment. He found himself in a moment in which he didn't know photography was going to be the career he would do for the rest of his life.

"I was kind of in a mind-space where all my friends went to study and I didn't know what I wanted to do. Did I want to go into music? Am I going to do photography and I didn't do a lot of photography during that time," Pierre shares. "I think the reason for it was because I thought I would probably do photography or music on the side as a hobby. It was during that time I found it hard to be creative and to do creative things. It was very hard for me because I was just in a place in my life where I didn't know what I wanted to do. I don't know why, I think maybe I was depressed about my current situation and how things were not going the way I wanted it to."

"Also, I knew that it was at that time my parents were going to possibly get divorced, and they've only recently been divorced. I think during that time I was very sad and kind in a space where I couldn't be creative. Thinking back I should have probably started creating more and more. That's the way I express myself, so I should probably just done more around that. Because when I arranged a shoot, it was great when I finished a shoot and I start editing photos and I enjoy it. But before the shoot, I'd be like, 'ugh, do I want to shoot now? Do I want to do this?' So I enjoyed it, but it wasn't as much as I do now," he confesses. "Now when I go, I'm super excited before a shoot. Especially if it's for a client I want to give them something they're happy, especially when they're paying."

Through this learning process, Pierre has also been able to realize that his wonderful work should be compensated. Even though he would feel scared of not being able to deliver a well-produced product, Pierre realized that his talent was the reason why they had hired him for the shoots. Through moments of realizing he had to purchase a new camera to fulfill his client's expectations to know the amount of editing, Pierre has been able to find a clear path of his work. From asking fellow South African photographers what they charge to having the support of his friends who supported his work and sharing his talent with others.

The latest project he has done was also made through his connection with choir and friend that recognized his talent and worth. Pierre worked alongside tenor singer, James Paradza to create a conceptual shoot for his opera singing poster that revolved on different forms of love. The result was a fascinating shoot that captured a beautiful dreamscape.

"In the future, I want to do way more of that, especially when it's just me doing something for the fun of it, where here he paid me and he was really happy with the photos. I was like, 'so I can do conceptual photography around a certain subject and get paid for it and make money with it.' Because always when you go into art, people tell you, 'well you're an artist and it's hard to make money.' And you always worry about that because living isn't free, so in terms of that, it's recently when I came back and I started shooting, it was visiting all those art galleries in Canada that I was like, 'I have to tell stories,'" Pierre shares.

"I don't like the business side of things. It's necessary for where I'm going, but it's very hard to think about that sometimes. Obviously for me as well, in photography, there is a price you can ask for certain things, but you also have to consider where you're at and how good you're in the situation the client wants to put you in. You have to consider things like that. That was hard, it was hard being that type of person and thinking the business side of things, where I just want to create and not think of that at all.," Pierre shares. "Because it's kind of awkward having your friends giving you money for what you do. One of my friends always says, 'Your friends should be the ones that pay you in full amount because they know what you're worth. Other people may not pay the full amount because they don't know how much you're worth.'"

Pierre's journey has just begun and his path to photography is only growing from here. It wouldn't be any surprise to see his work showcased in a fashion magazine or art gallery. As of this moment, it's truly an honor to share his beautiful photos on the pages of our Mother Nature and Home issues. His work has inspired me to continue pursuing my creative passion. For now, I highly suggest you follow him at @pierre.tography and if you find yourself in South Africa, don't hesitate in reaching out to hire him for a stunning portrait.

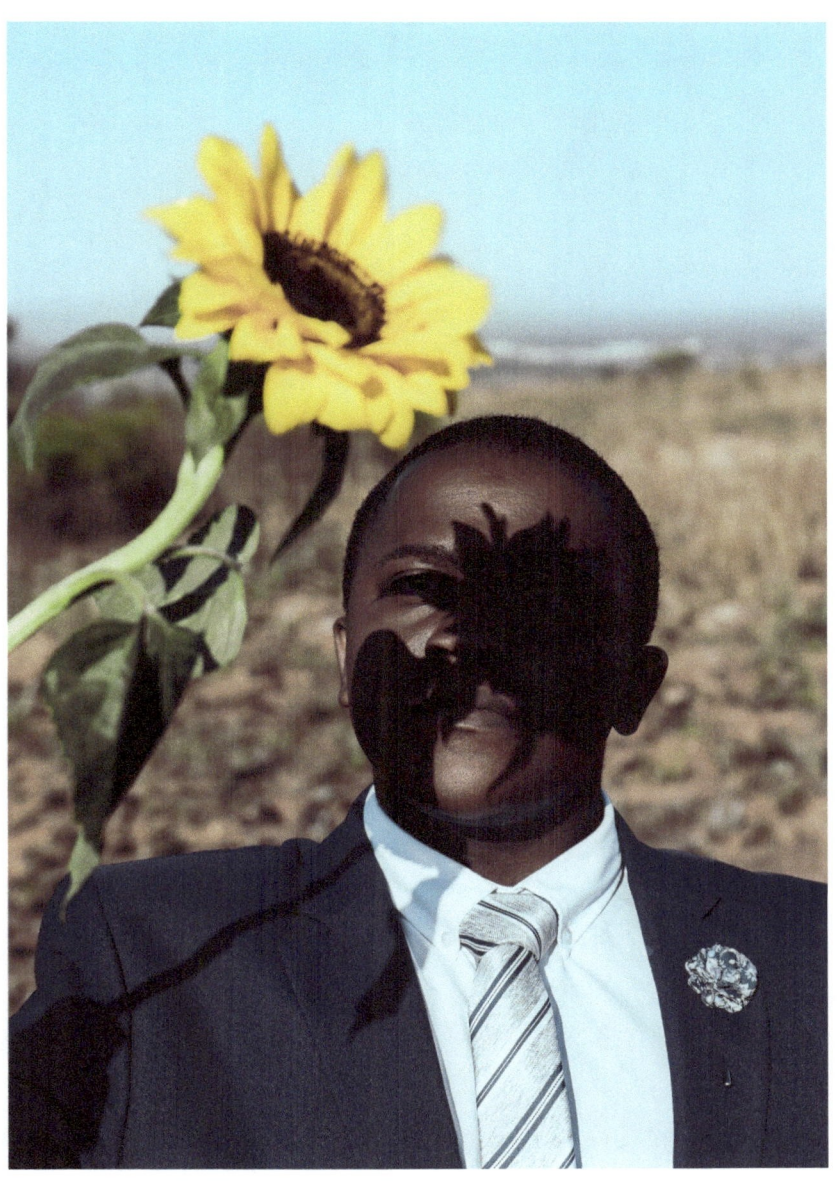

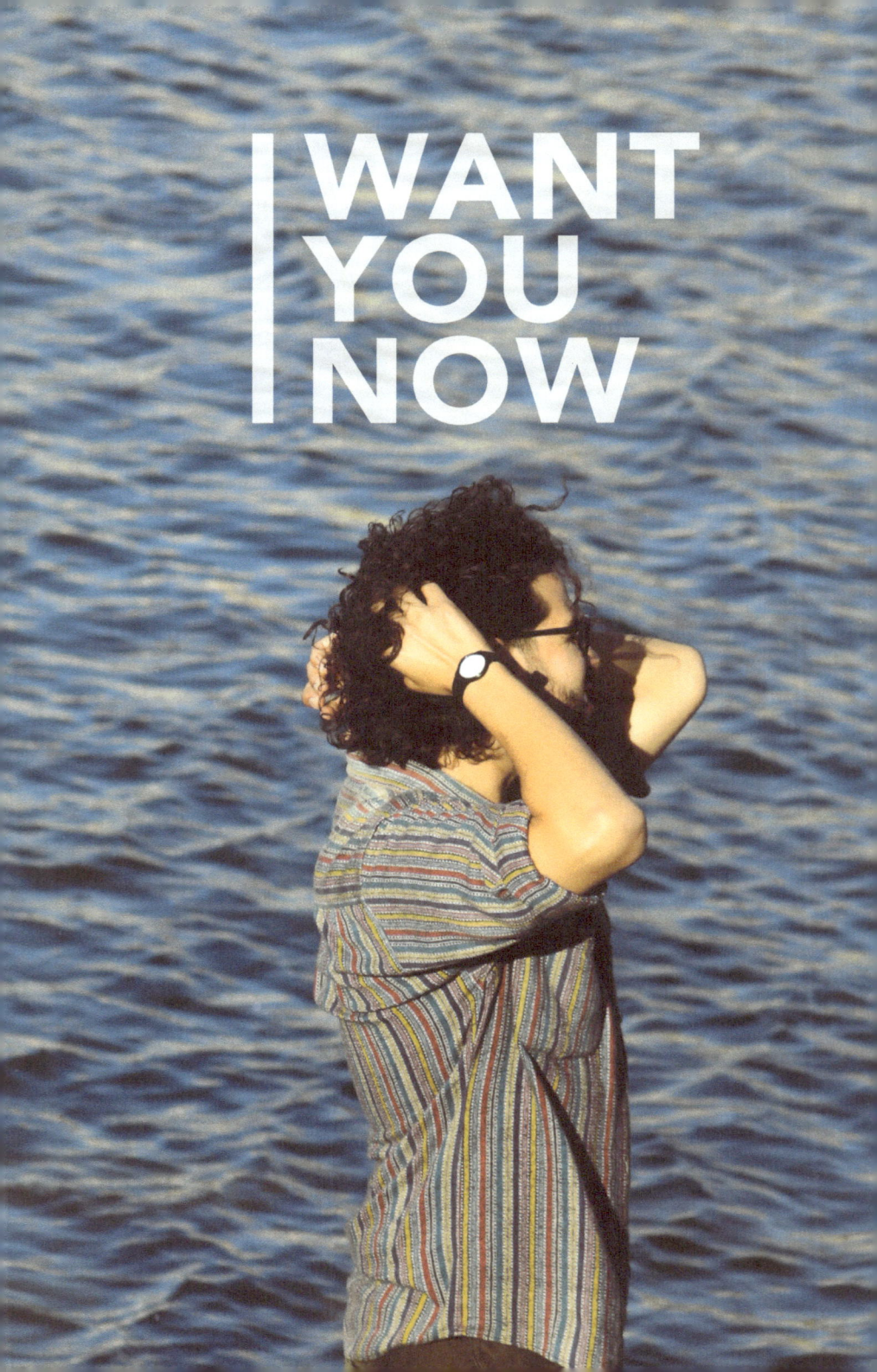

**I WANT YOU NOW
I WANT YOU TONIGHT
AND TOMORROW
MY LOVE**

RICHIE

I am satisfied with what you have for me.
All I need
in this time,
is to be with you
and near you
and loving you
without distance in between.

THE VICE COLUMN

Got It From My Mama

Josephine Jael Jimenez

My biggest goal in life is to not be my mother. Sounds unhealthy and slightly feasible, I know, but it's starting to become much more of a problem. Growing up, my mother's house was immaculate. Not just clean, which is obssessively was, but becautifully decorated with a steady rotation of in season decor. If that sounds magical to you, let me quickly tell you why it was a fucking nightmare with a single anecdote.

During Christmas, my mother goes all out on decorating her home. She has a massive Christmas tree that requires a ladder to decorate and elaborate garlands and wreaths that take up most of the garage to store. Every year, she changes the colors of ribbons that are interlaced because fake branches and she doesn't allow anyone to help her ever. That means that in all of my childhood, I wasn't allowed to decorate the Christmas tree. My dad used to buy us kids our own second tree to decorate, but he stopped after a year or two because my mother would just go back in and "fix" it anyway.

Needless to say, my mother has actual OCD, which I was then diagnosed with at a young age. From the very start, fate was trying to push me to be like her, but the house I grew up in was not a home. It was a model house, like the kind you see on new development lots. It was miserable. Especially considering the fact that we were not wealthy... at all. Any extra money were ever had went towards feeding my mother's desires and not into any type of savings account.

Cut to having my own home now and my own partner and my own still resurfacing OCD that I went to many years of therapy to try to curve and you'll fine a young woman trying so desperately not to have a model house instead of a home.

I demanded white dishes so I can see if they're dirty and white counter tops so I can see if they're dirty and white everything so I can see if everything is dirty and everyday I have to refrain from complaining that everything always gets dirty and that my partner, who does all the cooking, doesn't take the two seconds to wipe the fucking stove when he spills something as he cooks.

Yes, I'm a mess.

So I try to let things go. I let the donation pile linger longer than I would like and I don't pressure myself or my partner to do the dishes immediately after we use them. But my mother's house is still in my head and on the earth. I still hear her nagging voice telling us that we're all slobs in her biting Hispanic Mother tone. I've been told by others like me that it never goes away, you just have to ignore it.

And I really do have to, if only to break the toxic cycle of toxic homes where people couldn't be people and where kids couldn't sit on the living room furniture.

Brenda Hernández Jaimes, Editor and Head Writer, @bren_jai
Javier Covarrubias, @javi.cova
Josephine Jael Jimenez, Editor & Designer-in-Chief, @josietakestheworld
Marissa Black, @marissablackmail
Pierre Van Vuuren, @pierre.tography
Richie, @richiejamz
Young Ignorantes, @youngignorantes, youngignorantes.com

www.ingramcontent.com/pod-product-compliance
Lightning Source LLC
Chambersburg PA
CBHW040346220526
45473CB00009B/2801